Brian Wildsmith's
Favourite
Nursery Rhymes

OXFORD
UNIVERSITY PRESS

OXFORD
UNIVERSITY PRESS

Great Clarendon Street, Oxford OX2 6DP

Oxford University Press is a department of the University of Oxford.
It furthers the University's objective of excellence in research, scholarship,
and education by publishing worldwide in

Oxford   New York

Auckland   Cape Town   Dar es Salaam   Hong Kong   Karachi
Kuala Lumpur   Madrid   Melbourne   Mexico City   Nairobi
New Delhi   Shanghai   Taipei   Toronto

With offices in
Argentina   Austria   Brazil   Chile   Czech Republic   France   Greece
Guatemala   Hungary   Italy   Japan   Poland   Portugal   Singapore
South Korea   Switzerland   Thailand   Turkey   Ukraine   Vietnam

Oxford is a registered trade mark of Oxford University Press
in the UK and in certain other countries

British Library Cataloguing in Publication Data
Data available

ISBN: 978-0-19-272766-4 (paperback)

1 3 5 7 9 10 8 6 4 2

Printed in China

Paper used in the production of this book is a natural,
recyclable product made from wood grown in sustainable forests.
The manufacturing process conforms to the environmental
regulations of the country of origin.

Brian Wildsmith's
Favourite
Nursery Rhymes

OXFORD
UNIVERSITY PRESS

Georgie Porgie, pudding and pie,
Kissed the girls and made them cry;
When the boys came out to play,
Georgie Porgie ran away.

Humpty Dumpty sat on a wall;
Humpty Dumpty had a great fall.
All the king's horses and all the king's men
Couldn't put Humpty Dumpty together again.

Dickery, dickery, dare,
The pig flew up in the air;
The man in brown soon brought him down,
Dickery, dickery, dare.

Tom, Tom, the piper's son,
Stole a pig, and away he run.
The pig was eat, and Tom was beat,
And Tom went roaring down the street.

Ride a cock-horse to Banbury Cross,
To see a fine lady upon a white horse;
With rings on her fingers and bells on her toes,
She shall have music wherever she goes.

Hark, hark, the dogs do bark,
The beggars are come to town.
Some in rags, and some in tags,
And some in velvet gowns.

Mary, Mary, quite contrary,
How does your garden grow?
With silver bells and cockle-shells,
And pretty maids all in a row.

Hickety, pickety, my black hen,
She lays eggs for gentlemen.
Gentlemen come every day
To see what my black hen doth lay.

Little Boy Blue, come blow up your horn,
The sheep's in the meadow, the cow's in the corn.
Where is the boy that looks after the sheep?
He's under the haycock fast asleep!

Diddle, diddle dumpling, my son John
Went to bed with his trousers on;
One shoe off, the other shoe on,
Diddle, diddle dumpling, my son John.

Doctor Foster went to Gloster
In a shower of rain;
He stepped in a puddle, right up to his middle,
And never went there again.

There was a crooked man, and he went a crooked mile,
He found a crooked sixpence against a crooked stile;
He bought a crooked cat, which caught a crooked mouse,
And they all lived together in a little crooked house.

Bye, baby bunting,
Daddy's gone a-hunting,
Gone to get a rabbit skin
To wrap a baby bunting in.

Hush-a-bye, baby, on the tree top,
When the wind blows the cradle will rock;
When the bough breaks the cradle will fall,
Down will come baby, cradle, and all.

A cat came fiddling out of a barn,
With a pair of bagpipes under her arm;
She could sing nothing but, Fiddle cum fee,
The mouse has married the bumble-bee.
Pipe, cat; dance, mouse;
We'll have a wedding at our good house.

Hey diddle diddle,
The cat and the fiddle,
The cow jumped over the moon;
The little dog laughed
To see such sport,
And the dish ran away with the spoon.

The north wind doth blow,
And we shall have snow,
And what will the robin do then, poor thing?

He'll sit in a barn,
And keep himself warm,
And hide his head under his wing, poor thing.

Two little dicky birds
Sat upon a wall,
One named Peter,
The other named Paul.

Fly away Peter!
Fly away Paul!
Come back Peter,
Come back Paul.

Old Mother Goose, when
She wanted to wander,
Would ride through the air
On a very fine gander.

Mother Goose had a house,
'Twas built in a wood,
Where an owl at the door
For sentinel stood.

She had a son Jack,
A plain-looking lad,
He was not very good,
Nor yet very bad.

She sent him to market,
A live goose he bought,
Here, mother, says he,
It will not go for nought.

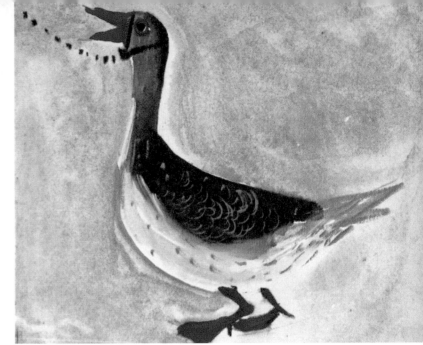

Jack's goose and her gander
Grew very fond;
They'd both eat together,
Or swim in the pond.

Jack found one morning,
As I have been told,
His goose had laid him
An egg of pure gold.

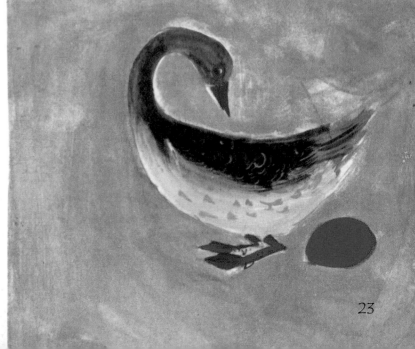

As I was going to St. Ives,
I met a man with seven wives,
Each wife had seven sacks,
Each sack had seven cats,
Each cat had seven kits:
Kits, cats, sacks and wives,
How many were going to St. Ives?

There was an old woman who lived in a shoe,
She had so many children she didn't know what to do;
She gave them some broth without any bread,
And whipped them all soundly and sent them to bed.

A dillar, a dollar,
A ten o'clock scholar.
What makes you come so soon?
You used to come at ten o'clock,
But now you come at noon.

Old King Cole
Was a merry old soul,
And a merry old soul was he;
He called for his pipe,
And he called for his bowl,
And he called for his fiddlers three.

Now every fiddler, he had a fiddle,
And a very fine fiddle had he;
Twee tweedle dee, tweedle dee, went the fiddlers.
Oh, there's none so rare,
As can compare
With King Cole and his fiddlers three!

Little Bo-Peep has lost her sheep,
And can't tell where to find them;
Leave them alone, and they'll come home
And bring their tails behind them.

Little Bo-Peep fell fast asleep,
And dreamt she heard them bleating;
But when she awoke, she found it a joke,
For they were still a-fleeting.

Then up she took her little crook,
Determined for to find them;
She found them indeed, but it made her heart bleed,
For they'd left their tails behind them.

It happened one day as Bo-Peep did stray
Into a meadow hard by,
There she espied their tails side by side,
All hung on a tree to dry.

She heaved a sigh and wiped her eye,
Then went o'er hill and dale,
And tried what she could, as a shepherdess should,
To tack to each sheep its tail.

This is the way the ladies ride,
Tri, tre, tre, tree,
Tri, tre, tre, tree;
This is the way the ladies ride,
Tri, tre, tre, tre, tri-tre-tre-tree!

This is the way the gentlemen ride,
Gallop-a-trot,
Gallop-a-trot;
This is the way the gentlemen ride,
Gallop-a-gallop-a-trot!

This is the way the farmers ride,
Hobbledy-hoy,
Hobbledy-hoy;
This is the way the farmers ride,
Hobbledy hobbledy-hoy!

One, two, three, four, five,
Once I caught a fish alive,
Six, seven, eight, nine, ten,
But I let it go again.
Why did you let it go?
Because it bit my finger so.
Which finger did it bite?
The little finger on the right.

Thirty days hath September,
April, June and November;
All the rest have thirty-one,
Except February alone,
Which has twenty-eight days clear
And twenty-nine in each leap-year.

One I love, two I love,
Three I love, I say,
Four I love with all my heart,
Five I cast away;
Six he loves, seven she loves, eight both love,
Nine he comes, ten he tarries,
Eleven he courts, twelve he marries.

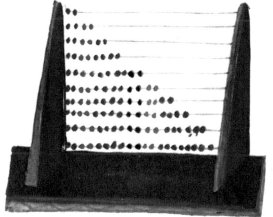

One, two, buckle my shoe;
Three, four, knock at the door;
Five, six, pick up sticks;
Seven, eight, lay them straight;
Nine, ten, a good fat hen.
Eleven, twelve, dig and delve;
Thirteen, fourteen, maids a-courting;
Fifteen, sixteen, maids in the kitchen;
Seventeen, eighteen, maids a-waiting;
Nineteen, twenty, my plate's empty.

Bobby Shafto's gone to sea,
Silver buckles at his knee;
He'll come back and marry me,
Bonny Bobby Shafto!
Bobby Shafto's fat and fair,
Combing down his yellow hair;
He's my love for evermore,
Bonny Bobby Shafto!

If wishes were horses
Beggars would ride;
If turnips were watches
I'd wear one by my side.

Pease-porridge hot,
Pease-porridge cold,
Pease-porridge in the pot,
Nine days old.
Some like it hot,
Some like it cold,
Some like it in the pot,
Nine days old.

What are little boys made of?
What are little boys made of?
Frogs and snails,
And puppy-dogs' tails,
That's what little boys are made of.
What are little girls made of?
What are little girls made of?
Sugar and spice
And all that's nice,
That's what little girls are made of.

31

Little Miss Muffet
Sat on a tuffet,
Eating her curds and whey;

There came a big spider,
Who sat down beside her,
And frightened Miss Muffet away.

Little Jack Horner
Sat in a corner,
Eating a Christmas pie;
He put in his thumb,
And pulled out a plum,
And said, What a good boy am I!

Pussy cat, pussy cat, where have you been?
I've been to London to look at the queen.
Pussy cat, pussy cat, what did you there?
I frightened a little mouse under her chair.

Wee Willie Winkie runs through the town,
Upstairs and downstairs in his nightgown,
Rapping at the window, crying through the lock,
Are the children in their beds?
For now it's eight o'clock.

A little cock sparrow sat on a green tree,
And he chirruped, he chirruped, so merry was he.
A naughty boy came with his wee bow and arrow,
Determined to shoot this little cock sparrow.
This little cock sparrow shall make me a stew,
And his giblets shall make me a little pie too.
Oh, no, said the sparrow, I *won't* make a stew;
So he flapped his wings, and away he flew.

Ding, dong, bell,
Pussy's in the well.
Who put her in?
Little Johnny Green.
Who pulled her out?
Little Johnny Stout.
What a naughty boy was that
To try to drown poor pussy cat,
Who never did any harm,
But caught the mice in his father's barn.

Three blind mice, see how they run!
They all ran after the farmer's wife,
Who cut off their tails with a carving-knife;
Did you ever see such a thing in your life?
As three blind mice.

Hot cross buns!
Hot cross buns!
One a penny, two a penny,
Hot cross buns!
If your daughters do not like them
Give them to your sons;
But if you haven't any of these pretty little elves
You cannot do better than eat them yourselves.

Three wise men of Gotham
Went to sea in a bowl;
And if the bowl had been stronger,
My tale had been longer.

A tailor, who sailed from Quebec,
In a storm ventured once upon deck;
But the waves of the sea
Were as strong as could be,
And he tumbled in up to his neck.

Solomon Grundy,
Born on a Monday,
Christened on Tuesday,
Married on Wednesday,
Took ill on Thursday,
Worse on Friday,
Died on Saturday,
Buried on Sunday:
That is the end
Of Solomon Grundy.

Pat-a-cake, pat-a-cake, baker's man,
Bake me a cake as fast as you can;
Pat it and prick it, and mark it with B,
Put it in the oven for baby and me.

In a cottage in Fife
Lived a man and his wife,
Who, believe me, were comical folk;
For, to people's surprise,
They both saw with their eyes,
And their tongues moved whenever they spoke!
When quite fast asleep,
I've been told that to keep
Their eyes open they could not contrive;
They walked on their feet,
And 'twas thought what they eat
Helped, with drinking, to keep them alive!

There was a little girl, and she had a little curl
Right in the middle of her forehead;
When she was good, she was very, very good,
But when she was bad, she was horrid.

Oh where, oh where has my little dog gone?
Oh where, oh where can he be?
With his ears cut short and his tail cut long,
Oh where, oh where is he?

A wise old owl lived in an oak;
The more he saw the less he spoke.
The less he spoke the more he heard:
Why can't we all be like that wise old bird?

There was a jolly miller once
Lived by the River Dee,
He worked and sang from morn till night,
No lark more blithe than he.
And this the burden of his song
For ever used to be,
I care for nobody, no! not I,
And nobody cares for me.

Cobbler, cobbler, mend my shoe,
Get it done by half-past two;
Half-past two is far too late,
Get it done by half-past eight.

Old Mother Hubbard
Went to the cupboard,
To get her poor dog a bone,
But when she got there
The cupboard was bare,
And so the poor dog had none.

She went to the baker's
To buy him some bread,
But when she came back
The poor dog was dead.

She went to the joiner's
To buy him a coffin,
But when she came back
The poor dog was laughing.

She took a clean dish
To get him some tripe,
But when she came back
He was smoking his pipe.

She went to the fishmonger's
To buy him some fish,
But when she came back
He was licking the dish.

The dog made a curtsey,
The dog made a bow;
The dame said, Your servant.
The dog said, Bow-wow.

If I had a donkey that wouldn't go,
Would I beat him? Oh no, no.
I'd put him in the barn and give him some corn,
The best little donkey that ever was born.

I saw a ship a-sailing,
A-sailing on the sea;
And, oh! it was all laden
With pretty things for thee.
There were comfits in the cabin,
And apples in the hold,
The sails were made of silk,
And the masts of beaten gold.
The four and twenty sailors,
That stood between the decks,
Were four and twenty white mice
With chains about their necks.
The captain was a duck,
With a packet on his back,
And when the ship began to move
The captain said Quack! Quack!

Jack and Jill went up the hill
To fetch a pail of water;
Jack fell down and broke his crown,
And Jill came tumbling after.

Then up Jack got and home did trot
As fast as he could caper;
And went to bed to mend his head
With vinegar and brown paper.

Simple Simon met a pieman,
Going to the fair;
Says Simple Simon to the pieman,
Let me taste your ware.
Says the pieman to Simple Simon,
Show me first your penny.
Says Simple Simon to the pieman,
Indeed I have not any.
Simple Simon went a-fishing
For to catch a whale;
All the water he had got
Was in his mother's pail.
Simple Simon went to look
If plums grew on a thistle;
He pricked his finger very much,
Which made poor Simon whistle.

John Cook had a little grey mare,
He, haw, hum!
Her back stood up and her bones were bare,
He, haw, hum!

John Cook was riding up Shuter's Bank,
He, haw, hum!
And there his nag did kick and prank,
He, haw, hum!

John Cook was riding up Shuter's Hill,
He, haw, hum!
His mare fell down and she made her will,
He, haw, hum!

The bridle and saddle he laid on the shelf,
He, haw, hum!
If you want any more you may sing it yourself,
He, haw, hum!

Dame, get up and bake your pies,
Bake your pies, bake your pies;
Dame, get up and bake your pies,
On Christmas day in the morning.

Dame, what makes your maidens lie,
Maidens lie, maidens lie;
Dame, what makes your maidens lie,
On Christmas day in the morning?

Dame, what makes your ducks to die,
Ducks to die, ducks to die;
Dame, what makes your ducks to die,
On Christmas day in the morning?

Their wings are cut and they cannot fly,
Cannot fly, cannot fly;
Their wings are cut and they cannot fly,
On Christmas day in the morning.

Monday's child is fair of face,
Tuesday's child is full of grace,
Wednesday's child is full of woe,
Thursday's child has far to go,
Friday's child is loving and giving,
Saturday's child works hard for a living,
And the child that is born on the Sabbath day
Is bonny and blithe, and good and gay.

Jack be nimble,
Jack be quick,
Jack jump over
The candlestick.

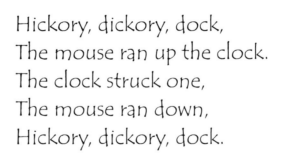

Hickory, dickory, dock,
The mouse ran up the clock.
The clock struck one,
The mouse ran down,
Hickory, dickory, dock.

Peter Piper picked a peck of pickled pepper,
A peck of pickled pepper Peter Piper picked;
If Peter Piper picked a peck of pickled pepper,
Where's the peck of pickled pepper Peter Piper picked?

If all the world were paper,
And all the sea were ink,
If all the trees were bread and cheese,
What should we have to drink?

Rain, rain, go to Spain,
And never, never, never
Come back again.

I love little pussy, her coat is so warm,
And if I don't hurt her, she'll do me no harm.
I'll not pull her tail, nor drive her away,
But pussy and I very gently will play.

See, saw, Margery Daw,
Johnny shall have a new master;
He shall have but a penny a day,
Because he can't work any faster.

Girls and boys come out to play,
The moon doth shine as bright as day;
Leave your supper and leave your sleep,
And come to your playfellows in the street.
Come with a whoop, come with a call,
Come with good will or not at all.
Up the ladder and down the wall,
A halfpenny roll will serve us all.
You find milk and I'll find flour,
And we'll have a pudding in half an hour.

Goosey, goosey, gander,
Whither shall I wander?
Upstairs and downstairs,
And in my lady's chamber.

There I met an old man
That wouldn't say his prayers;
I took him by the left leg,
And threw him down the stairs.

Four and twenty tailors went to kill a snail;
The best man among them durst not touch her tail.
She put out her horns like a little Kyloe cow;
Run, tailors, run, or she'll kill you all e'en now.

Charley, Charley,
Stole the barley
Out of the baker's shop.
The baker came out
And gave him a clout,
Which made poor Charley hop.

Little Polly Flinders
Sat among the cinders,
Warming her pretty little toes.
Her mother came and caught her,
And whipped her little daughter
For spoiling her nice new clothes.

Curly Locks, Curly Locks, wilt thou be mine?
Thou shalt not wash dishes, nor yet feed the swine,
But sit on a cushion and sew a fine seam,
And feed upon strawberries, sugar and cream.

Baa, baa, black sheep,
Have you any wool?
Yes, sir, yes, sir,
Three bags full:
One for my master,
And one for the dame,
And one for the little boy
Who lives down the lane.

Mary had a little lamb,
Its fleece was white as snow;
And everywhere that Mary went
The lamb was sure to go.

It followed her to school one day,
Which was against the rule;
It made the children laugh and play
To see a lamb at school.

And so the teacher turned it out,
But still it lingered near,
And waited patiently about
Till Mary did appear.

What makes the lamb love Mary so?
The eager children cry;
Why, Mary loves the lamb, you know,
The teacher did reply.

Where are you going, my pretty maid?
I'm going a-milking, sir, she said.
May I go with you, my pretty maid?
You're kindly welcome, sir, she said.
What is your father, my pretty maid?
My father's a farmer, sir, she said.
What is your fortune, my pretty maid?
My face is my fortune, sir, she said.
Then I can't marry you, my pretty maid.
Nobody asked you, sir, she said.

Little Tommy Tucker
Sings for his supper;
What shall we give him?
White bread and butter.
How shall he cut it,
Without e'er a knife?
How can he marry
Without e'er a wife?

Old Mother Shuttle
Lived in a coal-scuttle
Along with her dog and her cat;
What they ate I can't tell,
But 'tis known very well
That not one of the party was fat.

Old Mother Shuttle
Scoured out her coal-scuttle,
And washed both her dog and her cat;
The cat scratched her nose,
So they came to hard blows,
And who was the gainer by that?

The Queen of Hearts,
She made some tarts,
All on a summer's day;
The Knave of Hearts,
He stole those tarts,
And took them clean away.

The King of Hearts
Called for the tarts,
And beat the Knave full sore;
The Knave of Hearts
Brought back the tarts,
And vowed he'd steal no more.

Sing a song of sixpence,
A pocket full of rye,
Four and twenty blackbirds
Baked in a pie.

When the pie was opened,
The birds began to sing;
Was not that a dainty dish
To set before the king?

The king was in his counting-house,
Counting out his money;
The queen was in the parlour,
Eating bread and honey.

The maid was in the garden,
Hanging out the clothes,
When down flew a blackbird,
And pecked off her nose.
But there came a Jenny Wren
And popped it on again.

This little pig went to market,
This little pig stayed at home,
This little pig had roast beef,
And this little pig had none,
And this little pig cried, Wee, wee, wee!
All the way home.

Cross-patch,
Draw the latch,
Sit by the fire and spin;
Take a cup,
And drink it up,
Then call your neighbours in.

Jack Sprat could eat no fat,
His wife could eat no lean:
And so betwixt them both, you see,
They licked the platter clean.

O, the grand old Duke of York,
He had ten thousand men;
He marched them up to the top of the hill,
And he marched them down again!
When they were up, they were up,
And when they were down, they were down,
And when they were only half way up,
They were neither up nor down.

Peter, Peter, pumpkin-eater,
Had a wife and couldn't keep her,
He put her in a pumpkin shell
And there he kept her very well.

As Tommy Snooks and Bessie Brooks
Were walking out one Sunday,
Says Tommy Snooks To Bessie Brooks,
Tomorrow will be Monday.

Oranges and lemons,
Say the bells of St. Clement's.

You owe me five farthings,
Say the bells of St. Martin's.

When will you pay me?
Say the bells of Old Bailey.

When I grow rich,
Say the bells of Shoreditch.

When will that be?
Say the bells of Stepney.

I'm sure I don't know,
Says the great bell at Bow.

Here comes a candle to light you to bed,
Here comes a chopper to chop off your head.

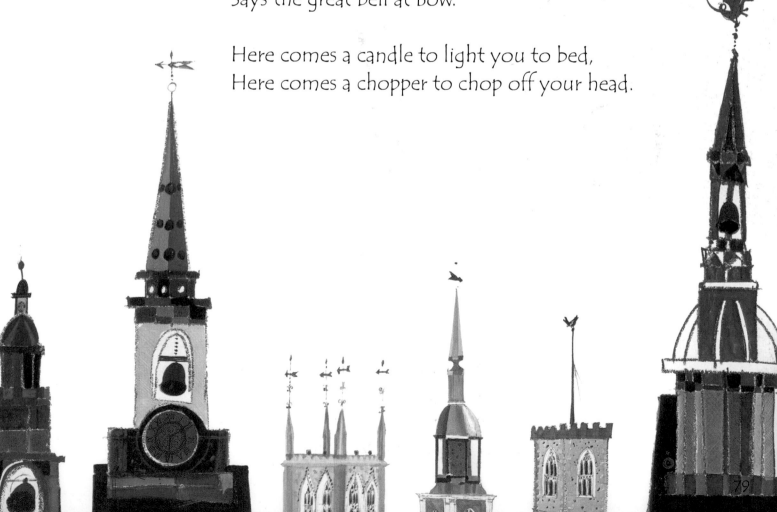

INDEX OF FIRST LINES